A ROUGH PAGE OF IMAGINATION

Sneha has a profound passion for writing and reading. Despite being at present, she is determined to chase her dreams and bring them to fruition. This book is a testament to her vivid imagination, evolving from rough drafts into a beautifully crafted collection now in your hands. Through her words, she invites readers into her world, offering a glimpse of her creative journey and aspirations.

My writing journey began with a simple poem,
'Ek Ladka hu Main' [I Am a Boy].
From there, my passion grew,
and I'm proud to present this book as a result of that journey.

A ROUGH PAGE OF

IMAGINATION

Fragments of Unfinished Thoughts

SNEHA PATEL

Disclaimer

This book is a translation of majority of poems originally written in Hindi.
The English version has been created with the help of online tools and resources. While every effort has been made to preserve the essence and emotions of the original work, some nuances may have been adapted to suit the language. The heart of these poems, however, remains rooted in their Hindi origin.

To my Mumma and Papa,

*Thank you for always supporting me, for
believing in me, and for being my constant source
of strength and encouragement.
Your unwavering love and guidance have been
the foundation of everything I do.*

With all my love,

Sneha

Prologue

In a world full of noise, poetry is where the heart whispers. These pages are not just collections of words, but echoes of thoughts, emotions, and moments that have touched the soul. Each poem holds a fragment of life's journey-love, loss, courage, and growth.

Through these verses, I invite you to pause, reflect,

and feel. Let the simplicity of words and the depth of feelings guide you through this landscape of emotions. Every poem here is a conversation, a story waiting to unfold, not just from me to you, but within you.

As you turn each page, may you find your own

meaning, your own reflection, and your own solace in the rhythm of these lines. This book is a piece of my heart, and now, it's yours.

This book reflects the raw, rebellious thoughts of a 15-16-year-old teenager—a young mind that dreams of a world filled with peace and support, where people stand by each other. Though she hasn't yet grasped all of society's rules, she values individuality deeply and refuses to bend to society's pressures.

Through these pages, she opens her heart and mind, exploring her feelings on society, nature, trends, love, and relationships, trying to understand them in her own way. Perhaps by seeing the world through this young perspective, you may gain insights into the hearts of teenagers and feel a stronger connection with them.[This book contains perspective of many teenagers].

{This book is a reflection of how that teenager feels every topic and emotion deeply.}

This poem reflects the growing obsession with materialism in today's world, where wealth and possessions define success. It questions the true value of chasing societal approval through material things while neglecting the environment and inner peace. I wrote this to highlight the need to pause and reflect on what truly matters in life amidst this rising culture of materialism.

1. THE MASK OF MATERIALISM

We're drawn to the shimmer of material things,
Caught in the spell of what wealth brings.
We measure others by what they own—
The latest gadgets, brands well-known.

We tell ourselves that success must show,
Through fancy cars and clothes on show.
But in this endless pursuit of more,
We forget the cost to our very core.

The earth grows weary, the harm runs deep,
In our greed, what promises can we keep?
We all desire riches, to shine so bright,
To impress the world in society's light.

But is it worth it—this grand charade?
What do we gain from the choices made?
Perhaps it's time to pause and see, What
truly matters to you and me.

This poem is a heartfelt conversation with Earth, highlighting its silent struggles and unending generosity despite human neglect. It portrays Earth's quiet sorrow as it provides us life and beauty while enduring the harm we cause. I wrote this to remind us of our responsibility toward the very planet that gives us everything, yet is often overlooked and taken for granted.

2. A CRY FOR CARE

Dear Earth, how are you doing today?

We rarely stop to think and harm you along the way.

But I want to ask, what's on your mind?

You give us so much, yet we leave you behind.

Your heart still beats, so strong and true,

Providing us life, the skies so blue.

But in your eyes, there's a sadness deep,

A quiet sorrow in the stories you keep.

The clouds carry your feelings; the rain begins to fall,

Like tears, as if you're crying, begging us to care for all.

You give us everything, yet we take and ignore,

Leaving your wounds open, we keep asking for more.

You try to guide us, to heal, to be free,

But we close our ears, and you whisper, "Why me?"

This poem reflects on the profound mystery of life and its meaning, a question no one can fully answer. It reminds us to cherish life as a precious gift, embracing joy, love, and kindness while letting go of greed. As a teenager, I often wondered what life truly meant, and this poem captures those reflections on its beauty and ever-changing nature.

3. A GIFT TO CHERISH

Life. What is it, really, when you think it through?

A mystery we all try to undo.

What does it truly mean? A question untold,

A puzzle too big for young or old.

Can anyone define it? I don't think anyone can,

To truly capture its essence, it's a challenge for man.

Yet, each of us sees it through our own eyes,

And in my heart, it's about living, no compromise.

We have one life, a gift from above,

Enough to be happy, enough to share love.

Those who've faced death and walked through the fire,

Understand life's value, its beauty, and desire.

One life to find joy, one chance to be free,

To spread kindness, to love, to just simply be.

But sometimes we get lost, chasing what we need,

And what we desire turns into greed.

Life whispers to us, to make each moment count,

Before it's too late, before the clock runs out.

So let's cherish it all, and live with grace,

For time moves quickly, we can't keep pace.

Live wild, live free, let your heart unfold,

Cherish each second, it's more precious than gold.

For in the end, it's not about what we've done,

It's about the love we've given, and the joy we've won.

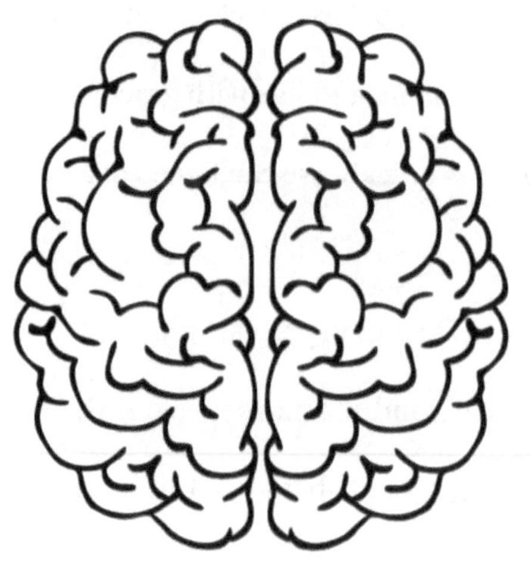

This poem is about discovering inner strength and realizing that self-belief is the key to unlocking one's potential. It reflects on a moment when I sat in my room, thinking about people who seemed far ahead in life, making me doubt myself. But then I asked, If they can achieve so much, why can't I? This thought inspired me to trust my abilities, embrace my journey, and keep striving for more.

4. UNLOCKING MY MIND

Locked in my room, I stumbled upon a key,

Not one made of metal, but one that set my mind free.

I realized in that moment, I've always had the power—

To choose my own path, to rise in every hour.

It wasn't about waiting for someone to believe in me,

It was about finding my own strength, setting my mind free.

Others might doubt, question what I can do,

But I've learned to trust my voice, my heart, my view.

If I choose to feel sad, I'll fall into that pain,

But if I choose to rise up, I can break through the strain.

I've come to understand, I'm not less than anyone else,

I'm just as worthy, just as strong, and full of myself.

I can take on the world with courage and might,

Chase my dreams, and let my soul take flight.

I'm capable of more than I thought before,

With each new step, I'm ready to explore.

So I'll keep trying, keep growing, keep pushing ahead,

Learning from the mistakes, and the paths I've led.

Every day is a chance, a new page to turn,

And I'll keep finding the lessons that help me learn.

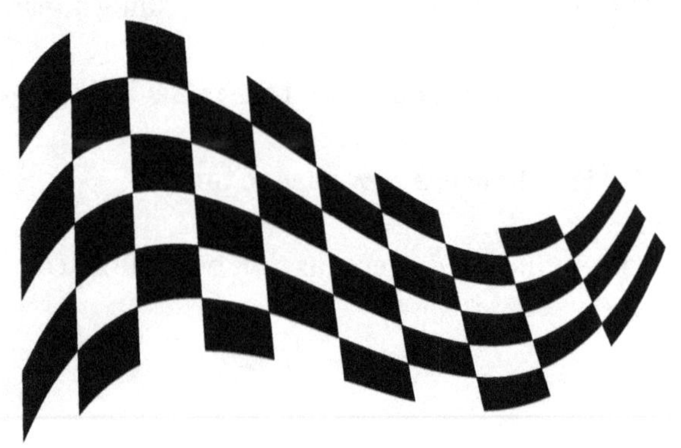

This poem is about the fire within to chase dreams and take control of one's destiny without waiting for the "right time." I wrote it after meeting a girl who, through her tears, reminded me that there's so much left to accomplish. While she spoke from an academic perspective, it made me see life as a whole—full of endless possibilities and responsibilities waiting to be fulfilled.

5. DESTINY IN MY HANDS

The day is slowly fading, and the night is drawing near,

But my dreams are far too grand to let time slip away in fear.

I won't play it safe or move at a slow, steady pace,

I'm here for the thrill, to take chances and leave my mark in this race.

The key to success is in my hands, and I won't wait,

I'll search for it, chase it, and claim it—no room for doubt or debate.

My dreams are locked away, hidden deep inside my mind,

Some belong to me, others not yet, but I'll make them all align.

I have responsibilities, duties that I must fulfill,

But my dreams call louder, and I won't let them stand still.

Life has been given to me, and I've learned to live with joy,

I won't rely on fate; I'll shape my destiny, starting today, not just a ploy.

This poem reflects the power of staying true to yourself despite the opinions and judgments of others. I wrote it when I realized how wrong it is to judge others, as being judged myself felt deeply hurtful. People often pass comments without considering the pain it causes. This made me think that before criticizing or judging someone, we should pause and empathize with how the other person might feel. The poem encourages listening to your heart and not letting the world's opinions dim your light.

6. RISE ABOVE THE NOISE

People's opinions are easy to voice,

But turning them into truth is a harder

choice.

It's easy to think what others believe,

But stopping those thoughts is what we

must achieve.

Listening to others and staying silent

may seem neat,

But hear today, and act tomorrow on

your own beat.

Listen to your heart and what it wants to

say,

If it feels right, don't let others take that

away.

If you can't forget their words, don't stray

from your way,

Because if you do, they'll still have their say.

If your hopes are shattered, don't expect

them to mend,

But don't let it break you, don't let it end.

People will try to stop you, push you

aside,

But don't bend, don't quit, keep your

pride.

Winning is your right, so shine with all

your might,

Let them say what they will, it's your time

to ignite.

This poem is a celebration of self-confidence and breaking free from shyness. I wrote it after meeting who girls who inspired me with their bold and confident attitude—they believed that if they wanted something, they could achieve it. It made me reflect on how I often held myself back, worrying too much about what others would think. This poem is a reminder to let go of those fears, embrace confidence, and trust in your own abilities to live life fully and fearlessly.

7. SHINE YOUR LIGHT

Let go of shyness, and let your confidence unfold.

In a world that's often selfish, trust yourself, be bold.

Stand tall on your own, support yourself through it all,

Don't rely on the opinions of others—trust your own call.

This world may try to push its own agenda, but don't let it take control.

Put it where it belongs, and let your spirit stay whole.

Walk with your head held high, with pride in your heart,

Ignore the gossip, let your light shine, play your part.

You've lived in pieces, now it's time to live as one,

Don't cry, smile at yourself, and have some fun.

Whatever comes to your mind, just let it be, Chase

your dreams, and set your spirit free.

You weren't truly living before, now it's time to thrive,

Learn to live fully, and let your soul come alive.

This poem reflects the whirlwind of emotions teenagers often face, with motivation being a key one. I wrote it to remind myself to embrace life, think differently, and keep moving forward despite criticism. Basically, it's a pep talk I gave myself—and hey, who better to hype me up than me.

8. TAKE THE LEAD

Life never stops, it keeps moving on,

Only how you live it matters, not the drawn.

Calendars show just dates, nothing more,

But the day you live life fully, becomes a historic score.

Just one perspective is needed to live,

People have fixed mindsets, about right and wrong to give.

But in this world, only those who think anew,

Succeed, with a "Can-do" attitude, shining through.

Don't worry about what's right or wrong,

It's up to you to decide, all along.

If everyone thought positively, the world would

be in harmony,

No wars, just love, a sweet melody.

Learn to think for yourself, show the world your might,

"I've done something, and can do more, I'm feeling
bright!"

When you take action, 90% will oppose,

But proving them wrong, depends on your inner glow.

People will talk, it's their job, they'll say,

But when you prove them wrong, your victory will sway,

Greater than any win, you've even known,

Believe in yourself, and make your spirit grown!

This poem captures the struggle of hiding emotions and the pressure of societal expectations. I wrote it because someone once told me I wouldn't understand what boys feel and how tough it is for them to express their emotions. It made me realize how important it is to give space for all feelings, regardless of gender.

9. *THE BOY BEHIND THE MASK*

I'm a boy, with emotions deep

But I'm told to hide, and never weep

I'm called sensitive, or momma's boy too

But I wish I could express, all my feelings too.

I put on a smile, and hide my tears

But inside I'm hurting, through all my fears

I wish someone understand, how I feel today

But I'm just a boy, trying to find my way.

I was taught to be strong, to never show pain

But now I wish I could, and break this chain

I'm human too, with feelings so real

But I'm stuck being a boy, with emotions to conceal.

I wish I could say, how I truly feel inside

But I'm afraid of being judged, and I cannot hide

So, I'll keep my emotions, locked deep in my heart

And hope that someday, I can be myself, and never depart.

A heartwarming poem about the growth and love of a family. Two birds build a nest, symbolizing the start of a family, which grows and flourishes over time. Despite physical distances, their hearts remain connected. The speaker reflects on the time and the blessings of their family life. They express gratitude for the love and connection they've experienced. The poem celebrates the joy and love of family, with all its ups and downs.

10. *UNSPOKEN THANKS*

Two little birds came from a far-off place,

Built a nest together with love and grace.

Our family grew as the children took flight,

Chasing their dreams, reaching new heights.

Though life scattered us far and wide,

Our hearts stayed close, always side by side.

I don't know when two turned to seven so bright,

And then seven became twenty-seven in sight.

Years passed by in laughter and delight,

It's hard to believe—it's been a beautiful night.

In my short 19 years, I never said "Thank you,"

But today, I feel grateful, more than I ever knew.

I'm lucky to call this nest my home,

A place filled with love, where I've never felt alone.

There were a few fights, but so much care,

In this home, we found a bond beyond compare.

This poem is for my best friend, who has always stood by me, motivating me through everything. It's for everyone who has a best friend— someone who celebrates your wins, wipes away your tears, and loves you unconditionally. A true best friend is a treasure that makes life whole, and this poem reflects that deep, unbreakable bond.

11. SOULMATE FRIENDSHIP

My best friend corrects me when I'm wrong,

And celebrates my wins with a happy song.

They know my secrets, my joys and my fears,

And wipe away my tears through all the years.

Their laughter is medicine that heals my soul,

With them, I'm never alone, I'm made whole.

They care for me deeply, with a love so true,

My best friend, a treasure, through and through.

They may get upset, but quickly forgive,

And with a smile, our bond begins to live.

My best friend is my heart, my shining star,

Together forever, near and far.

This poem was written for my cousin, with whom I share countless cherished memories. We only get to meet during vacations, and each time, we eagerly wait to be together again. From our dance competitions to silly fights, our bond is unbreakable, and she's not just my cousin but also my best friend. This poem captures the love and joy we share whenever we reunite.

12. SISTERLY LOVE

Hey sister, tell me, what's life like without me?

No messages, no letters—do you ever think of me?

Memories come rushing back, your quirky little ways,

Filling my heart with joy from our golden days.

Dance competitions where we ruled the floor,

I keep wondering—when will we dance once more?

Remember those silly fights, and how quick we forgave?

Our bond is unbreakable, the love we always gave.

You're not just my sister—you're my best friend too,

A treasure for life, always shining through.

A reflective poem about the year 2020, a time of unexpected challenges and growth. The poem expresses gratitude for the lessons learned and the transformative impact of the year's experiences.

13. LEARNING FROM THE JOURNEY

Year 2020, what a journey we've been through,

A time no one expected, yet it came true.

Thank you for the lessons, the growth, and the strife,

You taught me so much, and changed my life.

Initially, you seemed so harsh and unkind,

But after you left, I realized you were one of a kind.

Your presence helped me discover myself,

And understand the true meaning of life's wealth.

We always gave our time to others, never to ourselves,

But you showed us the value of self-reflection and self-health.

Year 2020, I learned so much from you,

Though I never thought I'd say this, but I'm grateful for you.

You were different, and we criticized you,

But now I see that you were one of the phases that happened to us, it's true.

You came to teach us valuable lessons.

To spend time with ourselves, learn new things, and find our true essence.

You helped us understand the importance of self awareness,

And how to appreciate the time we have, and make the most of it, with no regrets or resistance.

Year 2020, thank you for the lessons,

You taught me so much, with your presence.

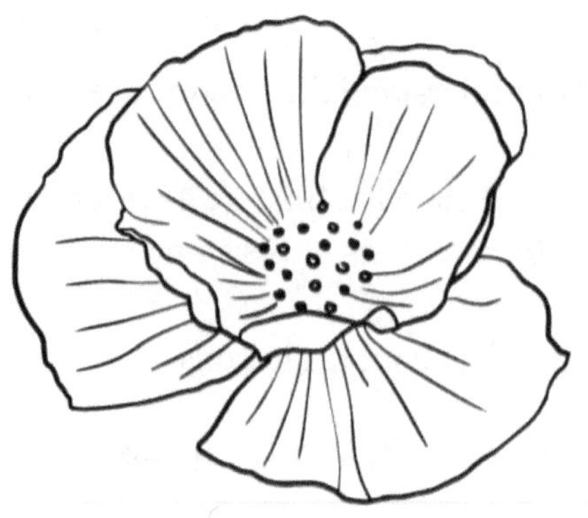

This poem reflects my journey of self-love and acceptance. I once wondered how I must have seen myself in the mirror all those years ago, and slowly, I discovered how I learned to appreciate and embrace myself. From the little joys of getting ready to the deeper connection with my inner self, this poem captures the love I've learned to cherish. It's a celebration of embracing who I am and knowing that this love will remain forever.

14. LOVE THYSELF

Seventeen years ago, I saw a glimpse of me,
A reflection so pure, it set my heart free.
I smiled at myself with endless delight,
Falling in love with my own radiant light.

Every laugh and every conversation I knew,
Made me cherish the person I've grown into.
With kajal and lipstick, a sight so bright,
I love myself more with each passing night.

No masks, no pretenses, just being true,
This love for myself feels ever so new.
Will it stay forever, deep in my heart?
Yes, I'll cherish it, never letting it part.

A heartfelt poem of self-discovery and empowerment, urging oneself to break free from fear and self-doubt. It encourages embracing flaws and letting go of the need for others' approval. The poem promotes self-love, acceptance, and confidence. It's a call to shine with one's true light and embrace individuality. A journey of self-discovery and growth.

15. A LETTER TO MYSELF

Oh, dear self, it's time to talk, No more
hiding—let's take that walk. Lost in others,
I've wandered too far, Now I want to find
out who you truly are.

I'm scared to face my fears, I'll admit,
And I've cried in silence, bit by bit.
I'm sorry for being so harsh and unkind,
Trapping myself in the maze of my mind.

Oh, dear self, take a moment to see,
Stop seeking approval, just let yourself be.
Yes, you have flaws, but who doesn't too?
Don't let fear define what's inside of you.

You wonder, "Can I truly shine bright?"
Or "Am I enough, even in my own sight?"
But it's not your flaws that bring the tears,
It's the whispers of doubt, the voice of your fears.

Let go of the weight, loosen the hold,

Your story is yours, so let it unfold.

You've denied your heart, but it's time to fight,

And know your worth—it's your birthright.

Oh, dear self, you're one of a kind,

The strength you need is already inside.

So take a stand, embrace your fire,

You're more than enough—let yourself inspire.

Stay bright, dear me, your journey's begun,

Shine on forever—you're your own sun.

This poem speaks to the deep longing for a connection with someone who truly understands, loves, and accepts every part of us. It expresses a desire for someone who doesn't need words to communicate but feels the connection through every glance and gesture. A person who accepts us, flaws and all, and stays through every high and low. It can be a romantic partner or a friend – someone who gives unconditional love and support. I wrote this because I've often wondered if there's someone out there who can truly see me for who I am and love me completely, with all my quirks, flaws, and strengths. It's a reflection of the human need for deep, unconditional love and acceptance.

16. NEVER ALONE

Someone, anyone, who understands me,
Loves me, wants me, and sets my soul free.

Someone who always holds my hand in harmony,

Without saying a word, just understands me.

And gets lost in my eyes, so bright as a sea.

Someone who fears losing me, you see,

Thinks only of me, and loves me with intensity.

And accepts everything about me, wild and carefree,

And stays with me, through joy and sweet melody.

And gets lost in my eyes, so deep as a sea.

Someone who thinks only of me, so true,

Listen to my nonsense, and sees it through.

And even appreciates the tasteless food I brew,

And waits only for me, with a heart so new.

And never ignores what I say, so pure and true.

Someone who waits only for me, so dear,

And with whom I can share all my hopes and fear.

And maybe it's true, that with them, I'll never shed a tear,

That with them, I'll never stop, and always hold them near.

And accept me with all my heart, so clear.

A heartfelt poem expressing a deep, soulful connection with loved ones, where secrets are shared, and true feelings are revealed. A beautiful declaration of love and trust, where the heart finds a peaceful and loving space, forever and always.

17. A BOND SO TRUE

Dear special one, you're the only one I trust,

With you, my secrets are safe, my heart adjusts.

The tears I hide, the fears I don't show,

You see them all, and yet, you never let go.

From the very start, it's been a magical ride,

With you, life feels like a dance on the tide.

My heart beats faster when you're in sight,

With you, my world feels beautifully right.

How do I describe this bond so rare?

A connection that words can't fully declare.

You've opened my heart in ways so new,

With every moment, my love only grew.

Hiding things feels heavy, it pulls me down,

But with you, I wear no mask, no frown.

You're my safe place, my guiding light,

With you, everything just feels so right.

Please know this love is deep and true,

Sometimes silence speaks louder too.

But one thing remains, steady and clear—

Forever and always, my heart stays near.

This poem expresses a love and connection so deep that no matter what happens, it remains unbreakable—like the bond between the sky and clouds, the moon and stars, or nature and its creations. It's for those rare and special people in our lives who we can never imagine leaving behind, no matter the circumstances. Whether it's our parents, friends, or a partner, these are the relationships that shape our world and make us feel whole. I wrote this for those who have such a strong place in our hearts, people we always want to be with, no matter what life throws our way.

18. BE WITH YOU

Always wants to be with you

Like the clouds never leave the sky

Always want to be with you

Just like how birds never stop flying.

Always want a relationship with you

Like the moon and stars

As the night feels incomplete without them.

Always want a life with you like nature

That changes but never abandons its creations.

Love Story

This poem captures the essence of a magical, perfect friendship or love story, inspired by the fairy tales we all grew up hearing or watching. Sometimes, we imagine a love so pure and joyful, just like the characters in those tales. I wrote this poem to reflect that dream—a beautiful connection with someone who always brings light and happiness into your life, no matter what. It's a fairy tale in its own way, where even the imperfect moments are part of a beautiful, unforgettable bond.

19. MY NEW WORLD

When I think of him, he always pops into my mind,
Taking me to a world so magical, so kind.
Where did he come from, quietly finding his place,
Becoming someone I could never erase.

He's the one who always makes me smile,
Appearing the moment I think of him, even for a while.
As time goes on, our bond gets stronger,
Full of laughter, and lasting longer.

My imaginary friend, who's always there,
A little spark of joy in the air.
From playful teasing to moments of cheer,
With him, there's nothing I fear.

Sometimes we argue, sometimes we laugh,
But every moment with him is like a perfect craft.
He's the thought that stays, so sweet and bright,
A magical friend who fills my world with light.

A heartfelt poem about a painful goodbye, longing for a lost love, and yearning for a second chance. It's an emotional cry to hold on to a fading connection, to understand and be understood, and to make the heart whole again. The poem expresses the intensity of love, the ache of loss, and the hope for reunion.

20. *THE WEIGHT OF GOODBYE*

I thought I had to let you go, but I can't seem to let it be,

Will you come back to me and help my heart feel free?

We never got the chance to meet each other's gaze,

And now, the time to part has come, in such unexpected ways.

The hand I longed to hold is now in someone else's care,

The shoulder I wanted to lean on, someone else will be there.

Do you know the weight of this ache I feel inside?

Do you sense the pain that I can no longer hide?

The eyes that were meant to comfort me through years,

Will they ever return to wipe away these fears?

It seems like you're walking away too soon, leaving me so bare,

If I let go, will you come back and show me you still care?

Four years together, and they passed like a fleeting dream,

Now each day feels endless, as though nothing's as it seems.

Forget the years, just stay with me a little while more,

Revive the love we had, and let my heart soar.

Things don't feel the same anymore, and I don't know why,

Is it the same for you, or am I the only one left to cry?

I'll wait for you, holding on to what we had,

Will you return and bring the joy we once had?

Will you come back, heal the hurt, and make our hearts fly?

Or is it truly the end, with no reason left to try?

Acknowledgements

I am deeply grateful to everyone who has supported me throughout the creation of this book.

First and foremost, I would like to thank my people for unwavering encouragement and belief in my dreams. Your support has been my foundation and my inspiration.

To Sudarshan and Kanika, thank you for your invaluable feedback and guidance. Your insights have helped shape these poems into their final form.

A special thank you to Notion Press for Printing this book which has been instrumental in bringing this collection to life.

Lastly, I am grateful to all the readers who will join me in this journey through these pages. Your openness to exploring emotions and experiences is what makes writing truly meaningful.

Thank you all for being a part of this journey.

Thank you To all my readers, thank you for picking up this book and allowing it to be a part of your journey. Your support and time

truely appreciated, and hope these words have brought happiness and insight into your life.

Thank you for being a part of this experience.

[If you are looking for Sneha… @sneha_p.19]

THANK YOU!

Questions

Self-Discovery Question

What did you learn about yourself during your teenage years?

Poetry-Specific Question

How did your teenage experiences shape your worldview and perspectives?

Creative Prompt

Write a letter to your teenage self. What advice or encouragement would you offer?